The problem of deer

poems by

Lydia T. Liu

Finishing Line Press
Georgetown, Kentucky

The problem of deer

ACKNOWLEDGMENTS

I am grateful to the editors at the following journals where earlier versions of
these poems appeared:

Cimarron Review, "I dreamed the problem of body."
Poetry Northwest, "December was a grassless month"
CHERRY MOON: *Emerging Voices from the Asian Diaspora*, "Antechamber"
Bellingham Review (83), "paean to hair"
Written Here and There: The Community of Writers Poetry Review 2020, "Fig"
Pigeon Pages, "Studies"
The Columbia Review (102:1), "the problem of deer in singapore"
Berkeley Poetry Review (51) and MIDTERM FOUR, "The problem of deer"

Publisher: Leah Huete de Maines
Editor: Christen Kincaid
Cover Art: Nicole Storm, copyright of Creative Growth Art Center
Author Photo: Stanley Fang
Cover Design: Elizabeth Maines McCleavy

Order online: www.finishinglinepress.com
also available on amazon.com

Author inquiries and mail orders:
Finishing Line Press
PO Box 1626
Georgetown, Kentucky 40324
USA

Contents

The problem of deer

Deer wander this place
warm to our   music

There is the problem of deer
 that is also the problem
of wander and the problem
of place that is also
the problem of music

The problem of deer is   is it   one
 or many
if many   how many
if one   how

is   perhaps   the problem   of our
 where i
am i

The problem of deer is   i
cannot give you deer   i
cannot give you deer if there is no
 deer
where there is no deer i
cannot make

The problem of music is   i can
make music   even
where there is no deer
in it   i can
make music   music
that is not deer   that
is not   there

The problem   there   is not the problem
 of where
deer is

  warm and   bloodied

1

The problem of deer in Singapore

and they want me from china in singapore

i am from china in singapore

my mother is from china in singapore
her mother is from china in china

mother is from modor in old english

modor is from the almost closure of the mouth

poem is from the almost closure of the mouth

i close my mouth in singapore

almost no deer in singapore

almost no from

Notes:

deer—wild sambar deer, once thought to be extinct in singapore since 1940. in the last decade have reappeared on highways in mandai, home to the singapore zoo and night safari.

home—there are 1.4 million migrant workers in singapore from south and southeast asia, many of whom work in construction and live in dormitories. as of 2020, the ministry of health in singapore tracks covid-19 cases in three categories: imported, community, and dorm.

english—in 2019 singapore celebrated the bicentennial of its founding by sir stamford raffles, a colonial administrator. one hotel, four schools, one hospital, and one station bear his name. two statues mark the civic district.

water—at 3 sen per thousand gallons from the johor river in malaysia. the agreement expires in 2061. a singaporean and a malaysian walk into a bar. they argue over the price of water.

sand—to reclaim land from surrounding sea, for a growing population. indonesia banned sand exports to singapore in 2007. sand mining in the coasts of riau, eastern sumatra, has destroyed 400,000 hectares of seabed and coral reefs.

singapore—from sanskrit (contested). lion city.

I dreamed the problem of body

The dream began in the afternoon.
The only way to write it was writing it.

There was San Francisco without a soul in it.

There was a gate.

The gate opened to the inlet.
The gate opened to the ocean.

In the dream the gate was open.

The souls rowed out.
To the last of the light.

To find themselves in the last of the light.

Under was Bicycle Rte. 2.
Under were no wheels. No legs.

A record store blasting *Under Pressure* to no one.
There was no one in the streets.

You only belonged in a place with nobody in it.
You only belonged in a body with no place in it.

In the dream the mallards passed as if the dream
         belonged to them.
In the dream the mallards were green and patient.

There was a time dimension to place.

At a certain velocity the bridge disappeared
         and there was only horizon.
At a certain velocity the horizon disappeared.

You sped toward a non-destination. Toward them.
Soul was emergent. A jazz.

You could not drive slow to this music.

-scape

Pink is the world turning
at its edge.

That with you
I am in. Like,

This.

Moon jellies rise
beneath the blue
mirror. One,
beached.

This part
of Oakland
feels like
Tuscany.

When asked

I answer *out of
town*, and
you, *here*.

Perhaps you are
a cypress.

I want
to be stationary

In a new
place.

Now am I

A balloon sculptor's
cormorant or

A sulfur hovering
Over sea waves or

Must we
be leaving—

In one origin story

You learn
Italian,

And we inhale
the yellow
of your

Nicotine.

I need to

Earn
things.

We need a permit

To place a soft
square
on this sand

Longer.

To sip salt water
In the noon sun.

Notes:

The Italian cypress is a transplant to dry, sunny California. Moon jellyfish swarm where they are carried by currents. The cloudless sulfur is native to the Americas (as is the tobacco plant); in the fall the butterflies migrate southward.

Studies (proem)

The green strobe of barricades.

Peeling paint
      on a footbridge.

The color of peaches left out for hours
           under the sun.

And the people on the grass.

Their bellies.

        Succumbing to gravity
          from all sides.

        Hairs thinned
over two seasons of loss.

Studies

the world today is half ocean half construction site

everywhere wide open

i walk into a taco bar and the waiter asks if i like this

i want to tell him touch me i'm made of water

the T takes me very slowly across the river

at the moment there is no other choice

frequencies are not real

even the semantics of our eyes are inconsistent

the tunnel went on and on pleased with its overtones

others have the loudness of their hands

if i can't be heard i'll look into your eyes blinking once for yes
      twice for indecision

what is the frequency of blue

irises are blue for the same reason as sky or ocean it is not a color
      you can have

have as in possess as in paint with

we were not in awe of likeness but of something close to study

viridian was mixed into her skin and sargent would paint water
      with the same longing

in the blue room i longed for blue

in the living room someone is talking about chinamen
        and their screaming children and dirty
        culture and in the same breath botticelli

sketching a yellow canary then i think about closeness as
        asphyxiation

there are no borders anymore

despite that i still have a chinese look about me

skilled as botticelli was he did not draw venus with both nipples

in other words we saw beauty in the unsaid

how i breathed you even apart

sound travels further submerged

at low frequencies waves compress the chest walls

everything is bluer than blue

the floor of the ocean its alkalis

how willing to move today as any other

Paean to hair

in the morning after
Lady Horikawa wrote about her tangled hair

later the poet ordained as a nun

in Barcelona I saw a painting
by Miró
        Hair Pursued by 2 Planets
or
            cabell   perseguit   per   dos
            planetes
in Catalan,

and bought it for
the bathroom

through metaphor I wield   a power I do not have

that weekend
Gloria
leaves
          "sea waste"
on the beach
of Barceloneta

what is the meaning of
clean,

every now and then a stray eyelash interrupts
my processes

the other day you tried
to google
immanence
in the sun
there was no internet

I liked your hair long

and dark
and even
how it does not mingle
with mine

how it creeps up your neck
like wisteria

        , trained
to the walls of that summer house

then lower
than you can see

slowly

strangling
its foundations

Studies (reprise)

in the last scene of *the godfather* after he tells kay
        who before that was appollonia
                who before that was kay
                        no they embrace

he surrounds her with his hands once more

                enter the cornet

you buzz your lips against the mouth
        of the cornet
                which replaces his hands

which are also from his father

the cathedral is a pair of right hands carved by rodin in 1908

about to clasp
the hands are intimate
        in a way that is
also impossible

if one thinks
about the feet

the chirality of a hand among other things explains
        why one remembers
                where one has been touched

Love after

—*after Derek Walcott*

There is still time
to choose elation.
Meanwhile   I will greet you   *friend*
open my port   *loving one* but also acquired *free*
in Celtic and Germanic in the sense of welcome
to set sail   *on the seas of this earth.* Be
you. I will love again a stranger who was yourself
            but will not tie my heart
to a jag of metal   *if there*

is where it needs to go. Ignore
the commandments.   I know nothing
if not my joy. Write the letters

and let them. Pin the notes
to the freezer door. Become the ocean
in the mirror. There is enough.

Fig

Upon returning from a walk and finding in my mailbox a letter from a man I'd loved, I was seized by a sudden and cosmic craving for figs. Fresh figs. Their scent of dew-covered milk-grass in the early hours of a mid-summer day, still cool from the breath of the night, their luminous pink flesh pregnant with a galaxy of celestial seed, enshrouded in a solemn purple that balloons like the foot of a Turkish şalvar and when penetrated overpowers the tongue with sweetness. I spent hours dreaming of them. In my dreams the figs were darker, richer, and more exquisite. A delicious longing filled the empty caverns of my mouth. I made no plans. It was as if my uncomplicated love had absolved me from a months-long yearning for raw fish,
a reminiscence of sweetbread,
a memory of first bite into hours-braised
pork belly at my childhood dinner table,
all that a father's love amounted to,
and the dull ache as I unlock the mailbox

a fig wasp
erupts—
wingless

and peer into the insatiable darkness of loin and gut. Loin and gut. In the Book of Rites, Confucius declared these the pinnacle of human desire, yet provided no further instruction.

Odors

After the war, most women found it impossible to leave the cities.
Maybe they believed the rocks still held the scent of the people.
—Mariana Oliver, tr. Julia Sanchez

Over time he came to learn that I smelled of "figs".

words for nostalgia in German: *Sehnsucht, Fernweh, Nostalgie,*
Wehmut, Heimweh[1]

coined by J. Hofer, a Swiss medical student, who
          rendered "an emotional phenomenon [Heimweh]
          into a medical phenomenon [nostalgia]" by translation[2]

from Greek *nostos* 'homecoming' and *algos* 'suffering, grief'

                              milky scents:
                              vanilla pods
                coconut pulp, coconut water
                  fig fruit sap, fig tree bark

"Long-term recognition memory is a special attribution of
olfaction, which shows an almost flat forgetting curve..."[2]

                              Consider: this of me
                        will be the last of him to go

                              Notes on Memoria[4]:
                  1, the expatriation of memory
                  2, vibrations buried in the sand
                  3, to the matrix she returns

Lectures on anthropology:
          "All senses have terms peculiar to them; for example, for
          sight these are red, green, yellow, for taste these are sweet,
          sour, and so forth. However, the sense of smell can have
          no terms peculiar to it, rather we take the terms from
          other senses. For example, it smells sour, or has the smell
          of roses, or carnations; it smells like musk. [...]

Consequently we cannot describe the sense
of smell."[5]

the fig leaf has a "sharp green scent,
grassy with a touch of bitterness"

A memory of a nose buried in the folds of skin.
He breathes deeply. The air as it leaves him condenses
into an untouchable quiet. A tree is to grow from this.

In this take, I do not ask for words, translations.
The silence is final and perfect.

[1]From "Özdamar's tongue", an essay by Mariana Oliver.
[2]Starobinski, Jean. "Le concept de nostalgie." *Diogène* 54 (1966): 92.
[3]Engen, Trygg. "Remembering Odors and Their Names." *American Scientist*, vol. 75, no. 5, 1987, pp. 497–503.
[4]*Memoria* (2021) is a film directed by Apichatpong Weerasethakul.
[5]Immanuel Kant. "Lectures on Anthropology." (1772)

First tongue

At first I am a body
floating in space.
A bag of marbles
with no shape to hold.
A cup of sunrise
added to a cup of sorrow.
The cup is made of violence.
The cup speaks   and I
am to act. I contort my body.
The body is a stage.
The stage is where I look
for what I have lost
in performance.
A performance of the mouth.
The mouth opens and at first
a tongue stands guard.
This is the first tongue.
It drinks from the cup.
The eruption of the second tongue
is violent, sudden, and full of cells.
It paints a bloodied picture
no one in the family
can read. It relishes the power
of performing
for an audience.
The first tongue grows quiet,
grows domestic,
banished to the kitchen.
It hoards flavors.
It reminisces
a discursive past. It is rediscovered
in third language, reenacted, translated.
It floats in a sea of
cellular memory.
It contemplates the implications of
saying, love, par
example, in the later tongues.

It holds back, that is to say,
it delegates its duties of expression.
It no longer commands. It is soft
and pliable and curious. It wants
to learn German. 例えば: Zungen.
Pflanzen. Like a new tongue
Lieben. peeling from itself.

Antechamber

other people have balconies.
        i don't have balconies.

there is a green beyond the window pane
under the season-less sun.

        i graft a guava tree
onto the mini-fridge.
i hold a fruit to your face.
you hold a screen to the red
in your sweater. it is cold
there. here is a
different compression
than bone to bone.

        a party
of eight will become
allowable. the shoulder
of a stranger will become
allowable. the chin. a touch
of their eye.

        i will exchange
this container for
a larger container
for a larger
container.

        i will inoculate
my dreams with
the after-now.

Sea change

Migratory birds stunned by glass
in the night the city's views are so
stunning just overhead the birds
pass by the thousands shadows
lost to the dark.

In the winter snowy owls fly south to New York.
Its climate resembles the arctic tundra.
You move to New York in December
to avoid the storms in February,
which never came.

December was a grassless month

So mā added grass to her name

because goats needed forage to live through
the long winter and mā was in labor
when the days were short and darkened
swiftly

                              It was the year of the goat, 2003.

That summer's grass sun-dried,
preserved in a prayer
spoken as she was called to dinner as child

                      May you have grass. Have you
your grass.

The character 韦
first seen during the 商 Dynasty
which came after the 夏, or summer,
pictured   a city
                              protected, or surrounded
: to defend, or disobey,
  or tanned animal skins,
  turned into bridle

With the addition of two leaves
                      of grass, 苇
referred to reed,
which was not only grass,
but grass that grew tall in an abundance of water
and remember that December
was a dry month.

What about the city then?
Probably because its defenders
were men of great stature
and the inventor of 字
had paddled a boat down a marsh lined
with reed and thought
                              "Great grass!"
or, for it was night,
mistaken the grass for very thin soldiers
defending the wetland.

Or a poet, encountering
a moment of the unsayable,
an aching love for the grass,
or burning wrath, depending
on whether the city was being protected
or under siege,
or perhaps each was the other's predicate
that is to say, they were one thing—
                              this grass, and this goat,
and this winter—
                        when this water
locked up in snow
and this thought of it   fell
                        on mā's parched tongue.

Upon arrival

I look at myself with a new strangeness.
        Who are you?

      •

In the dark
I cannot feel the size of my hands.

    •

A single bell chime
by moonlight.

•

      You are me.
I am everywhere.

     •

      Why have I come?
To hear the water.

Travel Poems

(Memory)

The first night
A. and I
lying in our hammocks
face to face with the stars.

She's named for lights.

I count at least two hundred
in this corner
she said.

Earlier at the airport
she'd lost everything
and now she was a child again
south of the Mediterranean

the same shadow of the olive trees
the endless wait
for one relative or another
who was visiting to show up
alive and so many meteors
would rain across the sky so many nights
they would stare and stare
sleepless.

The air smelled as it does now
of memory.

A single star falls
as we were speaking.

(Suspension)

In the cave
her hollowed out suitcase
hangs above
like a specter

consumed
by the terror of our futures
we lie open eyed
in the hotel room

this deep watery cave

the rocks about to
rouse from their dreams

are only now
inanimate

(Premature departure or the failure to arrive)

She fills a form at the lost and found

to enter the international database
of mishandled bags.

She browses the vacation shop
for forms to cover her hairless body.
Forms
fly out the drawers.
She laughs
then cries at
"100% polyester"
wonders
where her body will burn
after she dies.

A. has a form that is no longer recognized
by the international committee of forms.

At the airport she will never visit
they are asking her bodies
to hand over their forms.

She is holding on to the last of their forms.

Over the next few days she will call
the international database
of mishandled bags.

She will sign her name into tiny forms.
She will not give up her body.

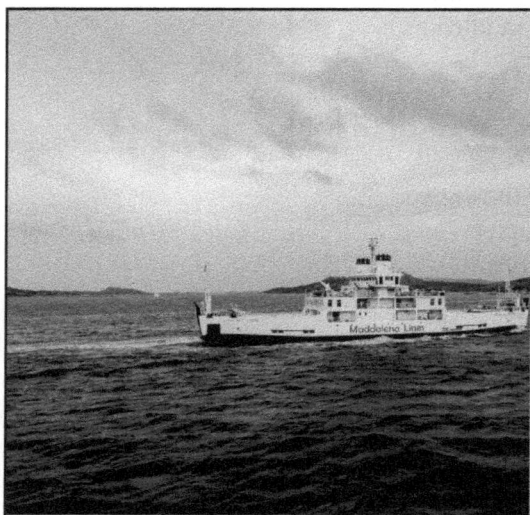

With Thanks

My deepest gratitude to teachers and poets who have shaped this book in one way or another: Shao Wei Chew Chia, María Gómez de León, Camille Dungy, Nicolas Freeman, Cecil Giscombe, Isabella Grabski, Robert Hass, Lyn Hejinian, Brenda Hillman, Major Jackson, Yeva Johnson, Bhanu Kapil, Hannah Kirwan, Jessica Laser, Ada Limon, Karen Llagas, Mary Mussman, Rachel Myers, Eileen Myles, Geoffrey G. O'Brien, Sandeep Parmar, Therí Pickens, James Richardson, Amy Shimshon Santo, Angela Siew, Susan Wheeler, Matthew Zapruder, and many others I have not named. The book will not be what it is without each of you. I'm grateful to the Community of Writers Poetry Workshop for nurturing this work, and the participants of various workshops I have had the privilege of sharing poems with over the years.

I'm grateful to dear friends with whom I have shared travels, dreams, and solitudes over the course of working on this book. You're the first readers of my life, and so much more.

Thank you, Mom and Dad. You've moved oceans and mountains, to me.

Lydia T. Liu (婷若) was born in Xi'an, China and raised in island city-state Singapore. Her poems have appeared in *Poetry Northwest, Cimarron Review, Berkeley Poetry Review* and elsewhere. A graduate of Princeton University and University of California Berkeley, she teaches at Princeton and lives in New York City. *The problem of deer* is her first chapbook.